NOTE

This work was written for the National Federation of Women's Institutes and was given its first performance by massed choirs of the Federation at the Royal Albert Hall on June 15th, 1950.

Acknowledgements :

Thanks are due to the following for permitting the use of copyright words and/or tunes :—

Messrs. Boosey & Hawkes Ltd. :
" God Bless the Master "
from *English Traditional Songs and Ballads*
edited by L. E. Broadwood.

Messrs. Cramer & Co., Ltd. (London):
" In Bethlehem City "
and " May Day Song " (2nd tune)
from *English County Songs*.

Messrs. Novello & Co., Ltd. :
" The Lark in the Morning "
" The Cuckoo "
" Sheep Shearing "
" John Barleycorn "
" The Unquiet Grave "

The Vocal Score is published separately

Orchestral material is available on hire

PROLOGUE

TO THE PLOUGHBOY

(For All Voices with Semi-chorus Descant)

Folk-song

Arranged by
R. VAUGHAN WILLIAMS

I SPRING

1 EARLY IN THE SPRING

For Three Voices (unaccompanied)

Folk-song

Arranged by
R. VAUGHAN WILLIAMS

9

Folk Songs of the Four Seasons

segue

2   THE LARK IN THE MORNING

(Two Voices with accompaniment)

Folk-song

Arranged by
R. VAUGHAN WILLIAMS

Moderato tranquillo ♩ = 100

17 bars
Instrumental ★

Grazioso

SOPRANO *p*

ALTO *p*

1. As __ I was a __ walk-ing one morn-ing in the Spring, I __ heard a pret-ty
2. The __ lark in the __ morn-ing doth rise from her __ nest, She __ mounts in the

dam - sel __ most sweet-ly to sing, And __ as she was __ sing-ing, these words she did __
air __ with the __ dew round her breast. It's __ all the day __ long she will whis - tle and __

say, "There's no life __ like a plough boy's all __ in the month of May!" _____
sing, And at night she will re - turn to __ her __ own __ nest a - gain. _____

say, __ "There's no life __ like a __ plough - boy's all __ in the month the month of
sing, __ And at night she will re - turn to __ her __ own __ nest a - gain, a -

Pfte.

___ May!" _____
gain. _____

★NOTE : When this song is sung alone these seventeen bars should be omitted

Folk Songs of the Four Seasons

3 MAY SONG

(For Full Chorus and Semi-chorus unaccompanied)

Folk-song

Arranged by
R. VAUGHAN WILLIAMS

O we've_ been_ ramb-ling all_ this_ night And some part
of this_ day,_____ And_ now we_ have re-turned a-gain And have brought you a
branch of may._____
A branch of _ may we've brought to _ you, And at your
door it_ stands,_ It_ is but a spray, but it's bright and gay By the work of_
our Lord's hands. Ah_____ Ah_____

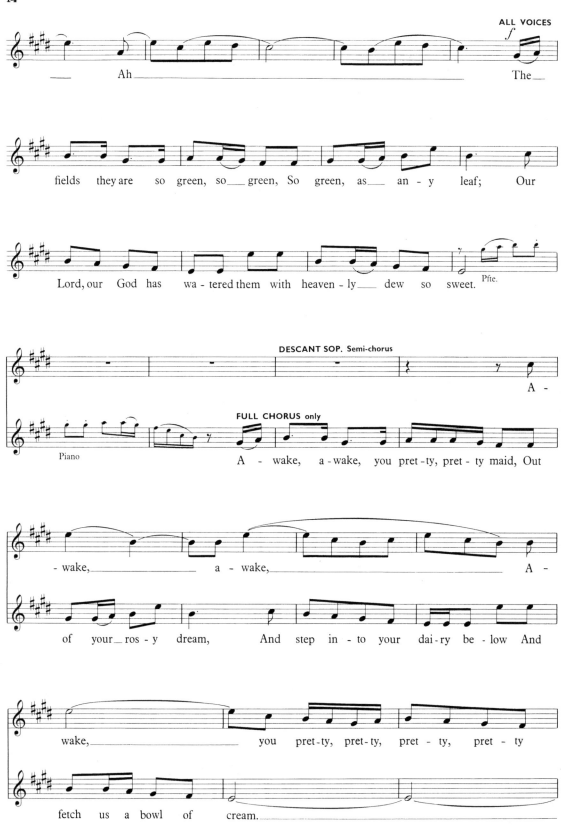

ALL VOICES

Ah___ The___

fields they are so green, so___ green, So green, as___ an-y leaf; Our

Lord, our God has wa-tered them with heaven-ly___ dew so sweet.

DESCANT SOP. Semi-chorus

A -

FULL CHORUS only

Piano

A - wake, a-wake, you pret-ty, pret-ty maid, Out

- wake,___ a - wake,___ A -

of your___ ros-y dream, And step in-to your dai-ry be-low And

wake,___ you pret-ty, pret-ty, pret-ty, pret-ty

fetch us a bowl of cream.___

maid.   Pfte.

DESCANT

Our song is done and we must be gone, No long - er

ALL OTHER VOICES

Our song is done and we must be gone, No long - er

can we stay, So God bless you,

can we stay, So God bless you all, both great and

great and small, God bless you all, both

small, And we wish you a joy - ful May.

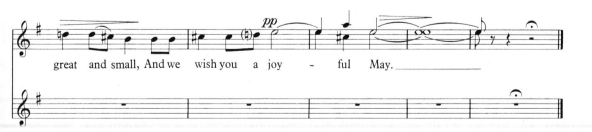

great and small, And we wish you a joy - ful May.

II SUMMER
1 SUMMER IS A-COMING IN
and
THE CUCKOO

(For Full Chorus and Semi-chorus, four parts)

Folk-song

Arranged by
R. VAUGHAN WILLIAMS

FULL CHORUS

NOTE : The first of these melodies is an adaption of the famous 'Reading Rota' which though nominally composed by John of Forncete is undoubtedly a setting of a folk-tune.

2 THE SPRIG OF THYME

(Two Voices with accompaniment)

Folk-song

Arranged by
R. VAUGHAN WILLIAMS

NOTE: The arranger cannot trace the source of the above version of this well known melody, he hopes that no copyright has been infringed.

red,__ I gath-ered the rose__ so dear, I__ gained but the

soon; The li-ly and pink I__ ov-er-looked And vowed I would wait till
me; But when I__ gath-ered the rose so dear I__ gained but the wil - low

v.4 only

wil - - - low tree,__

June.__   Pfte.   5. My gar-den is now run__
tree.__   wil - low__ it__ will__

DESCANT Verse 6 only

Green wil - low will twist,__

wild, When shall I plant it new? My bed that__ once was__
twist, Green wil-low it will twine; And I wish I was in that

1

will twine,__ That

filled with thyme Is__ all__ ov-er-run with rue.__ 6. Green
young mans arm's That__ once had the heart of mine.__

2

DESCANT   *pp*

once had the heart__ of mine.__

FULL CHORUS

mine, The__ heart__ of mine.__

Alternative for massed singing

mine.__   *segue*

Folk Songs of the Four Seasons

3 THE SHEEP SHEARING

For Two Voices unaccompanied

Folk-song

Arranged by
R. VAUGHAN WILLIAMS

all_____ to plough,_____ it's_ all_____

dance in a ring_ love,_____ When each lad takes his lass All

_____ to plough,_____ all_____ all_____ to plough,

on the green grass, And it's all_____ to plough_____

And it's all_ to plough Where the

_ Where the fat ox-en graze low,_____ And the lads and the

cresc.

fat ox-en graze low,_____ And the lads and the lass-es to_

lass-es to_ sheep shear-ing go, And it's all_ to

sheep shear-ing go._____

plough where the ox-en graze low._____

segue

4   THE GREEN MEADOW

Unison (All Voices)

Folk-song

Arranged by
R. VAUGHAN WILLIAMS

*This replaces a missing line in the original

Folk Songs of the Four Seasons

III AUTUMN

1 JOHN BARLEYCORN

Full Chorus, (Unison) and Semi-chorus, (Two parts with accompaniment)

Folk-song

Arranged by
R. VAUGHAN WILLIAMS

Melody and some of the words from the collection of the late Cecil Sharp

3. So then he lay for three long_ weeks_ Till the dew from heaven did
6. We'll tip white wine in to_ a_ glass_ And_ scar-let in-to a

fall :_____ John Bar - ley-corn sprang up a - gain_
can,_____ John Bar - ley-corn and his brown bowl_

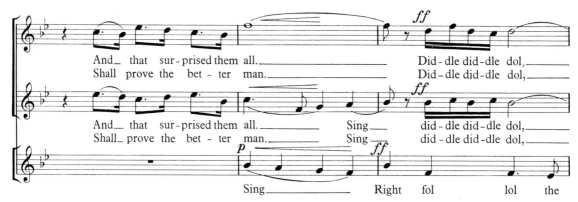

And_ that sur-prised them all._____ Did - dle did-dle dol,_____
Shall prove the bet - ter man._____ Did - dle did-dle dol,_____

And_ that sur-prised them all._____ Sing_ did - dle did-dle dol,_____
Shall_ prove the bet - ter man._____ Sing_ did - dle did-dle dol,_____

Sing_____ Right fol lol the

___ did-dle, did-dle did-dle, did-dle dol_____ the did-dle, right fol lee - ro

did - dle al the dee, right fol lee - ro

dee._____

dee._____

segue

2 THE UNQUIET GRAVE

(Three Voices unaccompanied)

Folk-song

Arranged by
R. VAUGHAN WILLIAMS

30

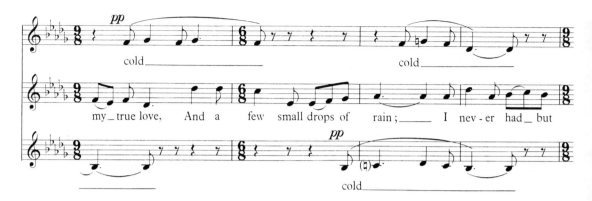

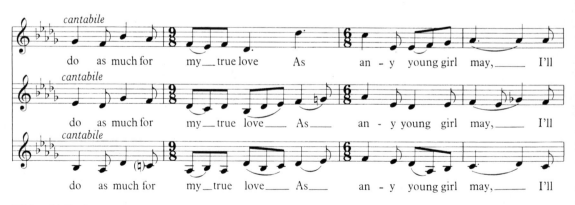

Folk Songs of the Four Seasons

Folk Songs of the Four Seasons

34

segue

Folk Songs of the Four Seasons

3 AN ACRE OF LAND

All Voices Unison

Folk-song

Arranged by
R. VAUGHAN WILLIAMS

IV WINTER
1 CHILDREN'S CHRISTMAS SONG

For Two Voices with accompaniment

Folk-song

Arranged by
R. VAUGHAN WILLIAMS

★ When this song is sung alone start here

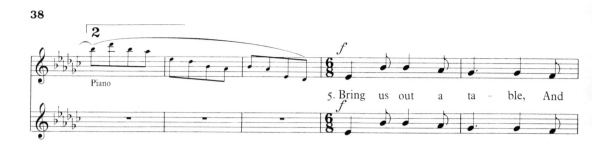

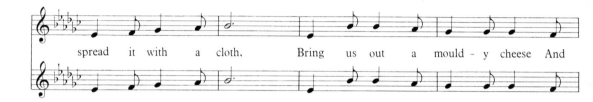

5. Bring us out a ta-ble, And

spread it with a cloth, Bring us out a mould-y cheese And

some of your Christ-mas loaf. For it's Christ-mas time, when we tra-vel far and

near; May God bless you and send you a hap-py new____

year,_____ May God send you a hap - - -

May God send you a hap-py, a

- - py, a hap-py new____ year._____

hap-py new____ year._____

2 WASSAIL SONG

For All Voices with Descant

Folk-song

Arranged by
R. VAUGHAN WILLIAMS

DESCANT

Was - sail___ Was - sail___ Was - sail

FULL CHORUS

5. Come but - ler, come fill us a bowl of the best,___ Then I pray your

Was - sail___

soul___ in heaven___ may rest, But if___ you___ do___ bring us a___

Was - sail___

bowl of the small, May the dev - il take___ but - ler, bowl___ and

Was - sail___ Was - sail___ Was - sail___

all!___ 6. Then here's to the maid in the

segue

3 IN BETHLEHEM CITY

For Three Voices (unaccompanied)

Folk-song

Arranged by
R. VAUGHAN WILLIAMS

merry, cast sorrow aside, our Saviour Christ Jesus was born on this tide.

merry, cast sorrow aside, our Saviour Christ Jesus was born on this tide.

merry, cast sorrow aside, our Saviour Christ Jesus was born on this tide.

2. But Mary's full time being come as we find, She brought forth her
4. Then God sent an angel from Heaven so high, To certain poor

first born to save all mankind; The inn being full, for the heavenly
shepherds in fields where they lie, And bade them no longer in sorrow to

guest No place could she find to lay Him to rest. Then
stay Because that our Saviour was born on this day. Then

Folk Songs of the Four Seasons

44

segue

4 GOD BLESS THE MASTER

(From the 'Sussex Mummers' Carol')

For all Voices with Descant last verse

Folk-song

Arranged by
R. VAUGHAN WILLIAMS

★ When this number is sung alone start here

Folk Songs of the Four Seasons

Folk Songs of the Four Seasons

OXFORD UNIVERSITY PRESS

Printed and bound in Great Britain by Caligraving Ltd, Thetford, Norfolk.

OXFORD
UNIVERSITY PRESS

www.oup.com

ISBN 978-0-19-387100-7

9 780193 871007